PREFACE.

In the pages of this Manual an attempt is made to give full and practical instruction in Sabre and Singlestick Play, and in the use of Sabre against Bayonet, and also to explain the course of practice that is necessary for those who wish to perform the difficult sword feats which require at once strength and lightness of hand. How far I have succeeded in what I have sought to do it will be for the readers of these pages to judge; but I may perhaps be permitted to say that the book which I now venture to offer to the public is the result of experience in the use of arms extending over an unusually long period, and that before I began to teach, some twenty years ago, I was so fortunate as to be trained by teachers of the highest skill. I learnt fencing from the late M. Prevost, Fencing-Master to H.R.H. the Prince of Wales, and to the Royal Family of France, and, as pupil and assistant, practised for many years with this admirable master of the small sword, who in his prime had been certainly one of the best fencers, perhaps the best, fencer in Paris. To make me as thorough a proficient with the weapon as he was himself, my esteemed friend spared no pains. In the use of the sabre and singlestick I was first trained by Mr. Platts, who had learnt from the celebrated Bushman his system of broadsword play. I thus had the advantage of learning from those best qualified to teach; but when, after no short or easy period of probation, I became in my turn an instructor, and gained that knowledge which can only be gained by teaching and by constant combat with adversaries of all degrees of strength, it appeared to me that that part of the course I had gone through had been somewhat conventional, and though the system of fencing which I had learnt from Prevost could scarcely be altered for the better, the English method of sabre play, good as it was, could be considerably improved. Sabre players, as a rule, have not been fencers, or at least have been fencers of trifling skill. Accomplished fencers have usually, from an exaggerated fear of losing their lightness of hand, not cared to work much with the sabre. The consequence has been that no attempt has been made to bring knowledge of the small sword to bear upon sabre play, and that little attention has been given to what is really the most formidable way of handling the latter weapon. Those who have taught its use seem to have thought of little else than the cuts which can be given with it, and to have overlooked the fact that the modern sabre, essentially a cut-and-thrust weapon, can be used with great effect for thrusts, and that, when thrusting, a man exposes himself less and is more likely to disable his antagonist than when he delivers a cut. It is true that one or two thrusts have been taught, but small reliance has been placed in them, and several of the fencer's methods of attack and defence which are admirably suited for sword play have been altogether neglected.

Daily combats gave me every opportunity for putting my ideas to the rough test of practice, and I soon found that I was not mistaken, and that there were longes and time thrusts which could be delivered with the sword, and were formidable even to the most skilled opponents. I made it, therefore, part of my work as a teacher and sabre player to improve sabre play by adapting to it many movements used in fencing which have hitherto been entirely overlooked by sabre players, and also by copying the fencer to make the attacks, &c., in a closer and consequently quicker and more effective manner than they had before been made.

These movements are specially described in this manual.

That the man who has mastered them will have a more varied and effective manner of using his weapon than one who has only practised the ordinary method, and will therefore be a far more formidable antagonist, will, I think, be admitted by all who, possessing some knowledge of the subject, do me the honour of giving attention to these pages; and inasmuch as sabre practice is not a mere exercise, but a course of training which teaches a man how to defend his life, it is scarcely necessary to point out that a really efficacious and not traditional method of using the weapon should be adopted. Recent events have shown our soldiers that even in these days of "arms of precision" the sword is not by any means obsolete. Assuredly these men should be taught to handle it in the best way. A soldier's life may often depend on his being able to wield his sword against a determined antagonist, and his chances of victory are not likely to be improved by the fact that his instructors have forgotten that a sabre has a point as well as an edge, and have not taught him the most formidable way of using the weapon they have placed in his hands.

It is true that to many of those who learn how to handle the sabre this matter is not of much importance, inasmuch as what they seek is a healthy and interesting exercise, and as they are not likely to have to wield the weapon in the defence of their lives. Considered, however, merely as an amusement and an exercise, sabre play is better when the conditions of the actual combat are followed as closely as possible in the mimic fight. It is more interesting and seems more real and practical, while the many varied movements which are required when every possible way of handling the sword is resorted to strengthen the whole frame as no other exercise can. I am not without hope that the altered system of sword play I have described in this Manual will, if properly followed, be found interesting by amateurs as well as by soldiers, and I am greatly encouraged in this hope by the fact that the very numerous pupils I have had the honour of instructing have never failed to take great interest in what they had to learn and practise : have often been as anxious to acquire complete mastery over the weapon as if they were shortly to use it in actual fight, and, in not a few cases, have attained exceptional proficiency. I would add that, while greatly changing the method of using the point in sabre play, I have been careful to retain all that was good in the old system, and have described minutely and to the best of my ability the established cuts and guards.

In these chapters I have written nothing special on Singlestick, as the stick is merely a substitute for the sabre, and is used exactly in the same manner, and throughout the Manual everything said about sword play applies equally to singlestick play.

On contests with sword against bayonet, nothing, so far as I am aware, has yet been written, and as the knowledge of how to use one weapon against another cannot but be of the greatest value to the soldier, I have endeavoured to put into the most practical form what I have learnt from observation of assaults innumerable, and from many hard struggles against vigorous antagonists.

Sword feats are of less importance than skill in the defensive and offensive use of the weapon, but when well performed are always greatly admired; and I have frequently found that good swordsmen were anxious to learn how to execute them. I have therefore carefully described the manner of accomplishing a variety of these *tours de force*. Some of these, such as—

Cutting a sheep in two at one stroke, and

Cutting an apple in a handkerchief without injuring the latter,

Are of my own invention, and I venture to say with confidence that any one possessed of a fair amount of strength, and accustomed to the use of the weapon, will be able, after some practice, to perform all the sword feats which are mentioned.

In conclusion, I trust I may be allowed, not in the usual formal manner, but as an assurance of respectful regard, to dedicate this little book to my pupils, whose attention and intelligence have yielded me unceasing encouragement, and to whose kind suggestion that I should put my system of instruction into a written form, these pages are due.

I have had the honour of instructing the following Clubs in both Fencing and Sabre :—

The London Fencing Club.
The Honourable Artillery Company, who, on my resignation after being with them upwards of twenty years, presented me with a very handsome testimonial.
The London Athletic Club.
The London Scottish V.R.C.
The 37th Middlesex V.R.C.
The 1st Middlesex Artillery.
&c., &c., &c.

The following gentlemen, all of whom were my pupils, have won the undermentioned prizes in open competition :—

1876.—London Athletic Club Cups for Fencing—1st. G. White, Esq. 2nd. R. Pullman, Esq.
1877.—London Athletic Club Cups for Fencing—1st. P. K. Rodger, Esq. 2nd. R. Pullman, Esq.

1877.—London Athletic Club Cups for Singlestick—1st. R. Hazard, Esq. 2nd. T. Wace, Esq.

1878.— London Athletic Club Cups for Singlestick—1st. H. H. Romilly, Esq. 2nd. R. Hazard, Esq.

1877.—German Gymnastic Society's Foils for Fencing—1st. H. Hartjen, Esq.

1878.—German Gymnastic Society's Foils for Fencing—1st. H. Hartjen, Esq.

1878.—German Gymnastic Society's Prize for Singlestick—1st. R. Hazard, Esq.

1879.—German Gymnastic Society's Prize for Fencing—1st. H. Hartjen, Esq.

J. M. WAITE.

19, BREWER STREET,

GOLDEN SQUARE, LONDON, W.

December, 1880.

LIST OF ILLUSTRATIONS.

SABRE.

PLATE		PAGE
I.	Preliminary position	16
II.	Engaging guard	18
III.	Feint at the head	26
IV.	A direct lead off at the head and guard (prime)	30
V.	Feint at the head and cut at the left cheek, and guard (quarte)	34
VI.	Feint at the head and cut at the left breast, and guard (prime)	36
VII.	Feint at the head and cut at the inside of the wrist	38
VIII.	Feint at the head and cut under right arm, and guard (high seconde)	40
IX.	Feint at the head and cut outside the leg, and guard (seconde)	42
X.	Feint at the breast and cut inside the leg, and guard	44
XI.	Shifting the leg to avoid a cut and counter on the head	46
XII.	Shifting the leg when a man attacks with his hand below the shoulder, and counter on the arm	48
XIII.	A draw and guard for shifting the leg and counter on the head or arm	50
XIV.	A draw and stop for shifting the leg and counter on the head or arm	52
XV.	Guard for an upward cut at the fork	56
XVI.	To deceive the beat under the blade (quarte thrust)	64

PLATE		PAGE
XVII.	Stop cut after deceiving the beat over the blade	66
XVIII.	Stop thrust (tierce) when a man draws his hand back to attack	69
XIX.	Time thrust with opposition	72
XX.	Time cut when a man raises his hand to attack	74

SABRE *v.* BAYONET.

XXI.	Engaging guard	94
XXII.	Parry of tierce	98
XXIII.	Parry of quarte	100
XXIV.	Cut inside of wrist after feint at head to deceive prime	102
XXV.	Cut at head after feint at inside leg to deceive half-circle	104
XXVI.	Thrust in quarte after feint in tierce. "One, two" to deceive tierce	106
XXVII.	Thrust under left arm after feint in quarte to deceive quarte	108
XXVIII.	How to seize the rifle after parrying prime	112
XXXIX.	How to seize the rifle after parrying quarte	114

SWORD FEATS.

XXX.	Lead cutting (before delivering the cut)	124
XXXI.	Cutting a sheep (after delivering the cut)	130
XXXII.	Cutting a broom handle on wine glasses	133
XXXIII.	Cutting a veil	136
XXXIV.	Cutting an apple on a man's hand	140

LESSONS
IN
SABRE, SINGLESTICK, &c.

HOW TO HOLD A SABRE.

IN holding a light sabre, place the fingers round the grip so that the middle knuckles are in a line with the edge, and let the thumb lie on the back to enable you to direct the point.

With a heavy sabre, the thumb should be placed round the grip, or you may be disarmed by a strong beat made with a sword of the same weight.

In singlestick, do not let the end of the thumb touch the hilt, or a hard blow on the hilt might seriously injure it.

Hold the sword securely, but do not grasp it tightly, or your hand and arm will soon tire. The grasp should only be tightened when delivering a cut or forming a guard.

There is great art in easing the grip directly after a movement has been executed. A swordsman who does this properly has what is termed "a soft hand," a great desideratum in sword play. It gives quickness to the hand, and saves it from being jarred.

PLATE I.—PRELIMINARY POSITION.

SABRE.

PLATE I.

PRELIMINARY POSITION BEFORE GOING ON GUARD.

Turn the left foot to the left, and place the right in front of it, so that the back of the right heel touches the inside of the left. The feet will then be at right angles. Easing the grip, let the back of the sword rest in the hollow of the right shoulder, the sword-elbow touching the right hip, and the hand in a direct line in front of it. Close the left hand, and place it on the back of the left hip (so that it cannot be seen from the front), with the elbow thrown back.

Body half turned to the left, face full to the front.

PLATE II.—ENGAGING GUARD.

PLATE II.

Engaging Guard.

Move the sword-arm to the front until the hand is directly opposite the hollow of the right shoulder, bend the elbow slightly and raise it, sink the wrist, and turn up the middle knuckles and edge of the sword. Advance, and lower the point until it is nearly opposite and level with the left hip.

Then advance the right foot about twice its own length straight to the front, and at the same time bend both knees *well*. Keep the body and head upright, and divide their weight equally between both legs, with the loins well pressed in.

When this guard is properly formed, the upper knuckles and elbow are level and in line with the shoulder. It is called *High Seconde*.

On crossing swords, which should be about nine inches from each other's point, when it is called an equal engagement, press your blade gently upon that of your adversary, so as to close the line in which you are engaged. By this means you are protected from a straight thrust.

I prefer this Engaging Guard to any other for the following reasons:—

That when properly formed, it protects the arm and body from all cuts, and the sword is in the best position to defend the head and leg, which may be done by merely raising and lowering the hand. In other guards you have to turn the point down in addition to doing so.

Simply raising or lowering the hand will also parry the thrusts, however high or low or at whatever part they may be aimed. Tierce and quarte, which are the other engaging guards usually taken, only defend the right and left breasts.

The hand and point are also better placed in it than in other guards for giving the stop thrusts and time thrusts by opposition, and all attacks except those directed at the head.

The Engaging Guard with the point up is, however, preferred and taken by some sabre players. It is called outside guard or *tierce* when the hand is on the right, and inside guard or *quarte* when on the left side of the body. In each of these guards one side of the arm is exposed, and for that and the above-named reasons I do not like either of them so well as the one with the point down (*high seconde*).

To form the Inside Guard or Quarte.

Place the right elbow about eight inches in front of the centre of the right breast, with the hand advanced and to the left. Pommel of the sword opposite the left nipple. The point as high as, and about two or three inches to the right (his right) of your adversary's right eye. Edge slightly turned to your left.

To form the Outside Guard or Tierce.

Move the hand about six or seven inches to the right without shifting the upper arm; which should be kept near the side, and slightly turn the palm down. Edge to the right. Point about two or three inches to the left (his left) of your adversary's left eye. Hand and point the same height as in Inside Guard.

These guards may be used as parries with good effect against a bayonet or lance.

An Engaging Guard formed in the manner above described is called "Defensive," as it covers the side on which you are engaged, and defends it from a straight thrust.

It is called "Offensive" when the arm is more straightened and the point directed to your adversary, so that the line in which you are engaged is open.

After engaging, you are not bound to remain with the blades touching, but it is an advantage to do so to a man who possesses a light hand and has a fine feel of the blade.

The feel of the blade often telegraphs to you your adversary's intention. By it you can tell if he is going to attack, or you may learn what guard he will form on the first movement of your attack upon him.

To obtain a proper feel of the blade, you should not grasp your sword tightly, but gently press the tips of your fingers on the grip, and keep as light a touch of your adversary's blade as possible.

To Advance.

Move the right foot about six inches forward, letting the heel touch the ground first, then let the left foot follow it the same distance.

To Retire.

Move the left foot back about six inches, and let the right follow it the same distance.

In advancing or retiring, keep the head and body erect and perfectly steady, with the knees well bent.

To Attack.

Stretch the sword-arm to its full length as quickly as possible on a level with the shoulder, without stiffness or jerking or any preliminary movement, and direct the edge or point of your sword to the part you wish to hit. Raise the toes of the right foot, and step straight to the front, until the feet are about four times the length of your foot apart; let the heel touch the ground first.

As you raise the foot to longe * press in the left haunch and straighten the left leg, keeping the left foot firmly fixed on the ground. In longeing, let the right heel almost touch the ground.

On the completion of the longe the body and head should be erect, the shoulders have their natural fall, and the right knee be perpendicular to the instep, left leg straight, and foot flat and firm on the ground, and the weight of the body equally divided between the haunches. The whole of these movements should be performed *together* with the greatest rapidity.

Be careful not to give any sign of preparation, but make the attack with great boldness and suddenness.

Do not raise the hand, or draw it or the point of the sword back when about to deliver an attack; by so doing you expose your arm to a time cut and the body to a time thrust.

In attacking, never let the foot touch the ground before the sword reaches its destination.

---

* Pressing in the left haunch when longeing adds considerable quickness to the attack, it also causes the body to be upright on the completion of the longe, and therefore enables a man to recover to the guard with less effort and greater quickness.

In all attacks and returns the point of the sword should travel over no more space than is necessary for it to arrive at its intended destination.

To Recover.

Draw back the arm and foot, and bending the left knee, resume the position of Guard, with knees well bent.

Opposition

Is to oppose your sword to that of your adversary when cutting or thrusting, either in an attack or return, so as to prevent him from touching you, at the same time in the same line, with a counter.

Thus if you deliver a cut on the left side of his head, bear your hand to your own left until it is as high as, and about four inches to the left of, your eye; the left side of your head will then be guarded.

In like manner, always cover with the forte of your sword the part of your own person which corresponds with the part you are attacking.

While cutting at your adversary's left side or thrusting with your palm turned up in *quarte*, your hand should be opposite your left shoulder. While cutting at his right side or thrusting with the palm turned down in *tierce*, your hand should be opposite your right shoulder.

The elevation of the hand depends on where the

attack is made, but it ought rarely to be below the shoulder, except when cutting at the leg.

Against a man who counters on the head, the hand should be kept as high as your own eye.

If you neglect your opposition you are liable to be both guarded and hit at the same time by a man who counters with good opposition.

PLATE III.—FEINT AT THE HEAD.

PLATE III.

Feinting.

A feint is a threatened attack made to induce your adversary to guard one part while you deliver the real attack on another. It is made by suddenly straightening the arm, without any movement of the body or feet, and directing the point at the place you wish him to guard.

Feints are also made to find out a man's method of defence and general style of play; when done for that purpose you should watch carefully what he does, and instantly return to your guard, but when it is your intention to follow up the feint with an attack the cut should follow the feint with the greatest rapidity.

An attack preceded by a feint is done thus: Make the feint as directed above, then longe, and by a quick and close action of the wrist, deliver the real attack, taking care not to draw back the hand as you do so.

This is called "Deceiving a Guard."

Guards.

All guards should be made with the edge of the forte of the sword, that is, the half of the blade next to the hand (the other half is called the feeble), and with the wrist well sunk. A firm guard is thus formed, and consequently a quick return can be given.

Too much force should not be used, so that a second guard may be readily made should the first be deceived. The sword should never be moved one inch more than is necessary to defend the part attacked.

PLATE IV.—A DIRECT LEAD OFF at the HEAD and GUARD (PRIME).

PLATE IV.

A Direct Lead Off at the Head and Guard.

This is the only direct cut in leading off that can be made with any degree of safety on a man who forms the engaging guard, shown in Plate II.

It can be given in five different directions, viz. :—

Horizontally, on the right side of the head.
    Ditto   on the left   do.   do.
Vertically.
Diagonally, on the right temple.
    Ditto   on the left temple.

I prefer the cuts on the left side of the head, for the reasons that the extra turn of the wrist necessary for their execution adds considerable force to them, and that when the opposition is correctly formed the whole of the head is defended from a counter, which is not the case when the cuts are delivered on the right side. Then the opposition only covers that side of the head. This I think to be of great importance, as the head, as a rule, is the part at which men naturally and generally counter. The vertical is not an effective one. A downward cut on the top of a man's head protected by a helmet would not do him much harm.

In making the horizontal or diagonal cut at the right side of the head, a man may be timed if his adversary, instead of guarding, gives a straight thrust with his hand opposite his right eye as the attack is being made. The opposition thus formed would guard the attack. This cannot be done on the cuts at the left side of the head, as there is no certain opposition on that side.

The diagonal cut at the left side of the head should be aimed at the temple in such a direction that, should the sword pass through, it would come out near the right angle of the jaw.*

It should be made with the wrist, and delivered in the manner described in page 22 (To Attack).

Be careful as you longe to bear your hand to the left, so that, as you strike the head, your hand is as high as, and a little to the left of, your left eye and look over your forearm.

GUARD FOR THE HEAD (PRIME).

Raise the hand until it is opposite the right temple, with the upper knuckles level with the top

---

* In actual combat I should aim the diagonal and horizontal cuts between the ear and the top of the jacket collar.

of the head, so that you can see under the forte of the sword without lowering the chin. Point well advanced, and nearly opposite to the left elbow, so as to cover the left cheek and breast. Edge upwards. Arm slightly bent, with elbow turned up and hidden behind the hilt.

A short man should form this guard a little higher than the right temple.

FEINT A STRAIGHT THRUST AT THE BREAST, AND CUT AT THE HEAD.

Feint a straight thrust at your adversary's breast under his blade, by suddenly straightening the arm, with the hand as high as the shoulder, and hilt turned upwards to protect the arm from a time cut; then, without lowering the hand or drawing back the point, longe and deliver the diagonal cut on the left temple.

This attack is sometimes made by feinting at the outside of the leg instead of at the breast. It is not, however, so safe, as you expose the arm to a time cut while making it.

PLATE V.—FEINT AT THE HEAD AND CUT AT THE LEFT CHEEK, AND GUARD (QUARTE).

PLATE V.

Feint at the Head and Cut at the Left Cheek and Guard.

This can only be done when a man forms his head guard with the point too high. Feint a cut at the head by straightening the arm and directing the point to a little above the centre of the forehead, edge of the sword turned downwards. Then, with the action of the wrist, and without touching your adversary's blade, pass the sword to your right until you have cleared his point, and with a longe deliver a cut on his left cheek just below the ear; the edge of the sword slightly turned up so that the arm may be covered with the hilt.

Opposition the same as in the diagonal cut at the head (page 31).

This cut may be given without being preceded by a feint, when the adversary forms his head guard with the point drawn back and high.

Guard for the Feint at the Head and Cut at the Left Cheek.

The guard for the head, described in page 32,

PLATE VI.—FEINT AT THE HEAD AND CUT AT THE LEFT BREAST, AND GUARD (PRIME).

will stop this attack, but should you find your opponent is passing his sword under your point, lower your hand quickly and bear it to your left until the pommel is opposite your left nipple. Point as high as the top of your head and a little to the left of your hand, edge to the left, wrist sunk, and inside of forearm resting on the body, to prevent the cut being given under the wrist.

This is the quarte guard with the hand drawn a little back. It may also be used against returns at the left breast.

PLATE VI.

FEINT AT THE HEAD AND CUT AT THE LEFT BREAST, AND GUARD.

This is done under the same circumstances and in the same manner as "The Feint at the Head and Cut at the Left Cheek," except that the cut is aimed at the left nipple. Opposition the same as when cutting at the head.

The guard, also, is the same, except that the hand should be a little lower when forming the quarte.

In this illustration the guard is formed with the point down (prime).

PLATE VII.—FEINT AT THE HEAD AND CUT AT THE INSIDE OF THE WRIST.

PLATE VII.

FEINT AT THE HEAD AND CUT INSIDE THE WRIST.

This is also done under the same circumstances and in the same manner as "The Feint at the Head and Cut at the Left Cheek," except that you only make a half longe, and aiming at the inside of the wrist, make a retrograde cut by drawing your hand towards your body, and at the same time retire out of distance to avoid the counter.

The guard for this attack is the same as the one for "The Feint at the Head and Cut at the Left Cheek."

None of the three preceding attacks can be made on a man who keeps the point of his sword well down and forward when guarding the head or left breast, and who does not attempt to return until he has found his opponent's blade.

The head guard, as described in page 32, will guard the left cheek and wrist, and the engaging guard with the edge a little turned to your left will defend the cut at the left breast. They should, as a rule, be used against all attacks directed against these parts.

The guard with the point up ought only to be used as an auxiliary, when you find that your point in forming the other guard has got too high.

If you always use it to defend the left side, you may easily be hit by a feint at the left and a cut at the right side or forearm.

PLATE VIII.—FEINT AT THE HEAD AND CUT UNDER RIGHT ARM, AND GUARD (HIGH SECONDE).

PLATE VIII.

Feint at the Head and Cut under the Right Arm, and Guard.

This attack, when well executed, is most difficult to judge and guard.

Feint at the head by suddenly straightening the arm and directing the point to a little above your adversary's forehead, with the edge of the sword turned down, then, without drawing back the arm, but with the action of the wrist only, longe and deliver a cut on the right armpit, the edge slightly turned up so that the arm may be covered with the hilt. Always aim this cut high, so that should your adversary form his guard a little low you will hit the outside of his shoulder.

Opposition, hand as high as and opposite to your right shoulder.

The cut may sometimes be given on the arm.

Guard for the Cut under the Right Arm.

Should you have been induced to answer the feint and form the head guard, lower the hand again as quickly as possible to the engaging guard, with the edge of the sword turned a little to your right.

PLATE IX.—FEINT AT THE HEAD AND CUT OUTSIDE THE LEG, AND GUARD (SECONDE).

PLATE IX.

FEINT AT THE HEAD AND CUT OUTSIDE THE LEG, AND GUARD.

This is done under the same circumstances and in the same manner as "The Feint at the Head and Cut under the Right Arm," except that you aim the cut at the leg a little below the knee, or you may make the feint by threatening a thrust at the breast over the blade.

Opposition to your right, and as high as possible.

GUARD FOR OUTSIDE LEG (SECONDE).

Drop the hand as low as the right hip and a little to the right of it. Point advanced as in the other guards and about 16 inches from the ground. Edge upwards.

PLATE X.—FEINT AT THE BREAST AND CUT INSIDE THE LEG, AND GUARD.

PLATE X.

A Feint at the Breast and Cut inside the Leg.

Feint a thrust at your adversary's breast over his blade, and as he raises his guard, pass your point to your right, and without touching his blade, clear his point and deliver a cut inside his leg above the knee with a longe.

Opposition to your left and as high as possible.

Another way of Attacking inside of Leg.

Beat your adversary's sword to your right, then suddenly straighten your arm, and turning the edge inwards, longe and deliver a cut on the inside of his leg.

Opposition to your left, and as high as possible.

Guard for Inside of Leg.

The same as for outside of leg, except that you move your hand to the left until it hangs over the right knee.

PLATE XI.—SHIFTING THE LEG TO AVOID A CUT AND COUNTER ON THE HEAD.

PLATE XI.

Shifting the Leg to avoid a Cut, and Countering on the Head.

As your adversary cuts at your leg, draw it quickly back and assume the first position shown in Plate I., and at the same time deliver a diagonal cut on his head or arm, with good opposition, so that should your adversary feint at your leg and cut at the head, the opposition will guard his attack. Be careful not to raise the hand in making the counter. This manœuvre may also be used against attacks made at the left breast.

PLATE XII.—SHIFTING THE LEG WHEN A MAN ATTACKS WITH HIS HAND BELOW THE SHOULDER, AND COUNTER ON THE ARM.

PLATE XII.

Shifting the Leg when a Man Attacks with his Hand Below the Shoulder, and Counter on the Arm.

The above manœuvre may be executed on any cut or thrust given with the hand below the shoulder, except that the counter should be aimed at the inside of the arm and the left foot moved back about eight inches before drawing up to the first position, so that you are out of distance.

The counter will act as a half circular parry should you not reach the arm.

The counter on the head or arm can also be given when a man returns at the leg after guarding his head. In this case you must recover in one movement from the longe to the first position, and at the same time deliver the counter.

It is much more difficult to recover from the longe than from the guard with sufficient quickness to avoid a return, but practice and good position on the longe will enable any one with good legs to accomplish it.

PLATE XIII.—A DRAW AND GUARD FOR SHIFTING THE LEG AND COUNTER ON THE HEAD OR ARM.

PLATE XIII.

A Draw and Guard for Shifting the Leg to avoid a Cut and Counter on the Head or Arm.

Feint a cut at outside leg, then longe, and forming the head guard, receive his counter on your sword and deliver a return under his right arm.

PLATE XIV.—A DRAW AND STOP FOR SHIFTING THE LEG AND COUNTER ON THE HEAD OR ARM.

PLATE XIV.

A Draw and Stop for Shifting the Leg to avoid a Cut and Counter on the Head or Arm.

Feint at outside of leg, and as your adversary tries to counter, make a half longe, and, aiming at the inside of his wrist, make a retrograde cut by drawing your hand towards your body, and at the same time retire out of distance.

Attacks at the leg should never be made without being preceded by a feint or a beat to divert your adversary's attention, and even when done in that manner you should be chary of their use. The man on the defensive has the advantage of either guarding and returning or shifting and countering, and should he adopt the latter method and not shift his leg quickly enough to avoid the hit, he would have considerably the better of the exchange.

I do not, however, think that attacks at the leg should be entirely ignored, neither do I think that they should always be avoided by shifting the leg. A man on horseback cannot do so. Both methods of defence should be practised. A man who relies entirely upon shifting may easily be drawn into a trap, as is shown in Plates XIII. and XIV. When mounted, the leg guards defend your horse as well as your leg.

Returns at the leg may be made without much fear of being countered.

FEINT AND CUT AT THE ARM.

Feint at the right temple and deliver a cut under the forearm, or feint at the outside of the leg and cut at the top of the forearm.

GUARD FOR THE ARM.

THE ENGAGING GUARD.

Should your adversary form his engaging guard with his hand higher than his shoulder, pass the point of your sword suddenly between his forte and wrist, and, turning the edge, deliver a drawing cut on the inside of his wrist, retiring out of distance as you do so.

PLATE XV.—GUARD FOR AN UPWARD CUT AT THE FORK.

PLATE XV.

GUARD FOR AN UPWARD CUT AT THE FORK.

This is not a good cut, and I do not recommend its use. To guard it, draw the right leg up to the first position, and at the same time form the outside leg guard.

STRAIGHT THRUST.

When on guard, the point of your sword is under the forte of your adversary's, and a straight thrust may be given should he quit the engagement, by suddenly straightening the arm and directing the point at his breast; deliver it with a longe.

A good time to make this thrust is when he prepares for his attack or dwells on his feint at your head, or when he advances, as described in page 59.

The guard for the straight thrust is the same as that used for guarding the outside of the leg.

THRUST BY DISENGAGING OVER THE BLADE.

This is given in the same manner and under the same circumstances as the straight thrust, except that you pass the point of your sword over the forte of your adversary's.

These thrusts may be given either with the palm of the hand turned down in tierce, when the hand should be opposite to your right shoulder, or with the palm turned up in quarte, when the hand should be opposite your left shoulder.

In both thrusts the edge of the sword should be well turned up, so that the hand and arm are covered by the hilt, and the point brought in line with the adversary's breast.

As the point touches, the hand should rise and the grip of the sword be slightly eased, the arm kept perfectly straight and well stretched.

It is dangerous to thrust when practising with sabres, unless you are well protected with pads; but with sticks the point should be freely used, always, however, taking care to ease the grip as the point touches, so that your hand may slip a little up the stick, and by that means avoid giving your adversary an unpleasant prod.

The guard for the thrust over the blade is the same as that used for guarding the head.

Feint a Straight Thrust and Disengage over the Blade.

Straighten your arm and threaten a straight thrust, and without bending the arm or drawing it back, disengage over the blade and deliver the thrust with a longe.

To Guard this Attack.

Form the outside leg guard, and then the head guard, as quickly, lightly, and closely as possible.

"One, Two."

Pass your point over your adversary's blade, and with a straight arm threaten a thrust, then, instantly, without bending the arm or drawing it back, pass your point under his sword and deliver a thrust with a longe.

To guard this attack, form the head guard and then the outside leg guard.

Attacks made with an Advance.

All the attacks can be preceded by an advance. When so done, the movement should be covered with a beat either under or over the adversary's blade, to prevent a stop thrust being given. The beat should be made very closely with the thumb and forefinger, and both it and the feint should be done while advancing, and the cut or thrust given with the longe.*

---

* The beat may also be used with great advantage in attacks not preceded by an advance. It should be made when a counter is expected, which it would most probably prevent, and should occasionally be used to check the adversary's parry.

In the advance and longe the right foot moves twice and the left once. They should move as quickly as it is possible to count " One, two, three."

A short man ought to use this method of attack when opposed to a tall man, as otherwise he cannot reach him. He should advance very rapidly, with short steps, and be prepared to parry as he goes forward should his beat be deceived.

A tall man ought seldom or never to advance when attacking.

RETURNS.

Returns should be made with a longe with the greatest rapidity after guarding. Great care must be taken not to draw back the hand or point before making them.

They should, as a rule, be made direct, but may sometimes be preceded by a feint, and should be very much varied.

The best returns from the different guards are the following, placed in the order of their comparative merits, that is, the first is a better return than the second, and so on; but their application should depend a great deal on your adversary's defence :—

From Guarding the Head.

Cut at the head.
Do. under the right arm.

Thrust at breast with palm down (tierce)
Cut at outside the leg.
  Do. left breast.
  Do. inside the leg.

From Guarding the Right Side under the Arm.

Cut at the head.
Thrust at the breast with palm down (tierce).
Cut under right arm.
      Do. on outside the leg.
      Do. on left breast.
      Do. on inside the leg.

From Guarding the Left Breast with the Point of the Sword down (Prime).

Cut at the head.
Thrust at the breast with the palm turned up (quarte).
Cut under the right arm.
      Do. at the outside of leg.
      Do. do. left breast.
      Do. do. inside of leg.

From Guarding the Left Breast or Left Cheek with the Point up (Quarte).

Thrust at the breast with palm turned up (quarte).

Cut at right cheek or neck (horizontal)
Do. at head (left diagonal).
Do. under right arm.
Do. outside of leg.
Do. left breast.
Do. inside of leg.

FROM GUARDING OUTSIDE OF THE LEG.

Cut at the right side of the head, neck, or shoulder.
Thrust at the breast (palm turned down).
Cut at the inside of leg.
Do. under the right arm.
Do. left breast.
Do. outside of leg.
Do. left horizontal at head. As you form the guard draw back your sword until it is clear of your adversary's point, and deliver a horizontal cut on the left side of his head.

FROM GUARDING THE INSIDE OF LEG.

Thrust at the breast (palm turned up).
Cut at the head.
Do. under the right arm.
Do. outside of the leg.
Do. left breast.
Do. inside of leg.

From Guarding the Thrust under the Blade.

Make the returns as from guarding outside of the leg.

From Guarding the Thrust over the Blade.

Make the returns as from guarding the head.
Returns at the arm should always be made when an opportunity is given.

STOP THRUSTS.

A stop thrust is given when a man advances with his attack. Immediately you see him move, deliver a straight thrust at his breast with a longe, you will then, if your movement is done in proper time, find your point on his breast as he has completed the advance, and he will be unable to longe and deliver his attack.

To prevent this thrust being made on you, beat under your adversary's blade as you advance.

PLATE XVI.—TO DECEIVE THE BEAT UNDER THE BLADE (QUARTE THRUST).

PLATE XVI.

To Deceive the Beat under the Blade (Quarte Thrust).

As your adversary advances with a beat, pass your point over the forte of his blade, and thus avoiding his beat, longe and deliver the thrust.

To Avoid This.

Instead of beating under the blade as you advance, pass your point over the blade and beat down.

PLATE XVII.—STOP CUT AFTER DECEIVING THE BEAT OVER THE BLADE.

PLATE XVII.

Stop Cut after Deceiving the Beat over the Blade.

As he advances with a beat over your blade, draw your arm back, and, avoiding his sword, deliver a cut at his head, or a thrust at his breast, with a longe.* This may also be done on a man who attacks your sword, or who makes short cuts at your head. On such occasions you must be careful to draw your hand towards your right temple, so that should he make a real attack your hand would be guarded.

Stop thrusts may also be used with great effect on a man who retires as you lead off at him, and then advances before making his return.

To do them under these circumstances, you must

---

* If it should unfortunately occur that you have to defend yourself with an ordinary stick against a man similarly armed, he will probably seek to disarm you by cutting at your hand. Deceive him by offering the hand, and on his cut, draw it back, and cut straight at his head. His blow will fall harmlessly, and the effect of yours will be considerably confusing to him.

be very quick on your legs, so as to be able to recover to your guard and deliver the thrust as he advances.

If you are not quick enough to do this, make a false attack with a half longe and draw him; you will then have more time.

To Draw the Stop Thrust and Stop Cut.

These may be drawn and parried thus : Advance as if you intended to attack, but instead of doing so parry the thrust and return quickly.

PLATE XVIII.

Another Stop Thrust used against a Man who Longes with his Arm Bent, or who Draws his Hand Back when Attacking.

Immediately you see him move, longe and deliver a straight thrust, or you may give the thrust without longing, by merely straightening the arm. I prefer, however, to longe with the thrust, as it is more certain to stop the attack.

Stop thrusts, to be successful, should be given without hesitation and with the greatest boldness.

PLATE XVIII.—STOP THRUST (TIERCE) WHEN A MAN DRAWS HIS HAND BACK TO ATTACK.

REMISE.

A remise is a sort of time hit made on the longe, when a man after guarding delays his return. It is done thus: Immediately after you have delivered your attack, draw your hand and head back to simulate a recovery, and without moving the foot, make a second hit at the same place as rapidly as possible.

Unless this hit is given decidedly before the return is made, the hit counts to the one who returns.

Renewal of the Attack or Redoubling.

A redouble is a renewal of the attack when your adversary after guarding does not return. It should be done with great rapidity and in a different line to that of the first attack.

REPRISE ATTACK.

A reprise is a sudden repetition of the attack, after a phrase in which no hit has been got and both have returned to the guard. It must be done with great quickness, so as to catch your adversary a little unprepared.

PLATE XIX.—TIME THRUST WITH OPPOSITION.

PLATE XIX.

Time Thrust with Opposition.

A time thrust can be made when a man feints at your head and tries to deliver a cut under your right arm, or on any part of the right side down to the foot.

As he raises his point to feint, make a straight thrust at his breast with a longe, keeping your hand as high as your right shoulder and a little to the right of it. Palm turned down.

Should you be quick enough, your point will fix on his breast, and his cut will fall on the forte of your sword.

If you are too slow, your thrust will guard his attack, although you may not touch him.

The same movements should be executed on the adversary, when from the engagement of *High Seconde* he endeavours to deceive prime, or, when from that of tierce, he tries to deceive quarte with "One, Two."

Another Time Thrust.

When from the engagement of quarte he attempts to deceive tierce by a "One, Two," lower your point on his first movement, and bearing your hand to your right, deliver a thrust on his right

PLATE XX.—TIME CUT WHEN A MAN RAISES HIS HAND TO ATTACK.

flank with a longe. Hand to your right and palm turned down.

To Draw and Stop a Time Thrust.

Feint a cut at the head or a thrust over the blade, and instead of delivering a cut or thrust, parry the thrust, and return with a half longe.

PLATE XX.

A Time Cut.

When a man raises his hand or draws it back to lead off, hit him on the outside of the wrist and get away out of distance.

In using the stop thrusts, remises, and time thrusts, great judgment is required. They should never be attempted until the swordsman has had considerable experience. When given at the proper time, they are beautiful and effective strokes, but when badly timed, great danger attends their use, and mutual hitting is often the result.

Young players will do well not to attempt them.

In an assault, should you find yourself timed and not know how to draw and stop a time thrust, your safest plan will be to make direct attacks only, that is, attacks not preceded by a feint.

DRAWING.

Is to induce your adversary to deliver a certain cut or thrust for which you are prepared. To do this, make a false attack, that is, attack with a half longe so that you can the more readily recover and guard; thus, having drawn out and guarded his cut, instantly deliver a genuine one.

To prevent this being done upon you, draw back your hand as your adversary makes his false attack, and thus avoiding his sword, deliver a cut on his head with a longe (*vide* Plate XVII.).

OBSERVATIONS ON FEINTING.

When a man makes a feint on you and you foresee his intention, do not answer it, but wait and parry his last movement. When acting on this principle, take care he does not make a direct attack, for should he do so, you will be too late, as his arm would be straight before you have moved.

If you answer a feint, form your first guard as lightly and as correctly as possible, so that you have time to make a second one.

By not forming the first correctly, your adversary, taking advantage of your fault, would be able to hit you when otherwise he could not. The hits shown in Plates V., VI., and VII. are got through this cause.

When you are in doubt about his intentions, step back out of distance on his first movement.

When a man will not answer your feints, make them with greater energy and rapidity, and thus force him to do so.

How to Deal with a Man who is Continually Countering.

When you meet with a man who is guilty of this very bad practice, you should deal with him in the following ways :—

Either act on the defensive and let him lead off, then after guarding, return as quickly as possible and get away.

Or, make false attacks, and thus draw out his counters, which guard, and then returning with great quickness, get away.

Or, by opposition, when, should his counters be directed at your head or left side, lead off without feinting with good opposition (in fact your opposition should be slightly exaggerated) at the part of his person which will correspond with that of your own at which you think he will aim his counter.

If his counters are directed at your right side, attack him with a straight thrust with your hand as high as, and a little to the right of, your right shoulder. Palm turned down.

When Opposed to a Man who Engages in Quarte or Tierce.

When opposed to a man who engages in quarte or tierce, you will find that he will guard his right cheek and side with tierce, and his left side with quarte. You may then make the following attacks in addition to those already shown :—

From the Engagement of Tierce.

Cut at the inside of his wrist.
Feint inside the wrist and cut at the outside.
Feint at the left cheek and cut at the right.
Feint at the left breast and cut at the right side or at his forearm.

From the Engagement of Quarte.

Cut at the outside of his wrist.
Feint outside the wrist and cut at the inside.
Feint at the right cheek and cut at the left.
Feint at the right side and cut at the left.

His stop thrust should be avoided in the following manner :—

To prevent him from giving you a straight

thrust as you advance to attack, beat his blade either in tierce or quarte.

Should he avoid the beat by disengaging and thrust upon you, make a beat before you move the feet, then, as you advance, change quickly and beat on the other side of his blade, and instantly deliver your attack.

The beat will probably draw his disengagement, and the change will parry it.

To change is to pass your sword under that of your adversary, and rejoin the blades on the opposite line.

OBSERVATIONS.

On Countering and Hard-Hitting.

When you are making an assault with sabres or sticks, remember they are substitutes for sharp swords, and act as though every hit you would receive would either kill or disable you. All your movements must be governed by this idea. You should never attempt to do anything with a stick that you could or would not do with a sword.

You must remember that in an actual combat the sabres have sharp points and edges, and that a very light touch would probably place you *hors de combat*.

Hitting at your adversary when he is attacking

you is almost as bad as cutting your own throat, for you are almost certain to be more or less seriously wounded; your chances of escape are very small indeed. You must, therefore, always endeavour to guard the attack and never counter except when you can avoid the hit by shifting.

You must never hit after you are hit, as it is very doubtful if you would be able to do so with sharp swords.

The act of countering, so deservedly popular among boxers, is not admissible here. A blow with the fist will probably only shake you, but with a sharp sword the effect would be much more serious. There is no such thing as give and take with that weapon, and I question if there is much in a serious encounter with sticks, as a well delivered blow on any part of the head would in all probability cause a cessation of hostilities.

Rough and heavy hitting should be avoided: it destroys quickness; greater effect is given to a hit by pace than by force.

A hard hitter has to brace himself together before attacking; he thus prepares, and while doing so may easily be hit.

If his attack is guarded, he cannot recover and guard a return so readily as he ought to do.

His returns are not given so quickly as they should be, for after guarding, he is almost certain to draw his hand back in order to make them with greater force.

As he hits, so he will guard; heaviness will pervade all his movements; therefore, if you deceive his guard, he cannot make a second one with sufficient quickness to stop a good attack, as he will throw too much force into the first.

Slowness is the natural result of heaviness, quickness that of lightness; therefore, if you wish to become a *bon tireur*, cultivate and practise light play.

In trying to play light, you must not get into the habit of making snatching hits by which you would only scratch your adversary. However lightly you deliver them, let them be so given that with a sharp sword they would be effective, and your points fixed so that they would penetrate.

CUT *versus* THRUST.

Some writers on the sword, acting on the presumption that the sword must be elevated in order to gain force before cutting, have asserted that the point traverses two-thirds less distance when thrusting than when cutting. If this were correct, the less use made of the cut the better, as a good swordsman would most certainly give a time cut on the arm or deliver a thrust on a man while he was thus preparing to cut.

I once saw a sketch drawn to prove this assertion, in which the man thrusting was depicted with his point lowered to a line with his adversary's breast instead of being level with his eye, while the man who was cutting, and should have had his sword similarly placed, had his point drawn back and raised about two feet above his head, a distance greater than I should draw the point of my sword back were I going to cut the carcase of a sheep in two at one stroke.

The point should not be drawn back or elevated when cutting either in an attack or in a return.

There is only one direct cut in leading off (that at the head), and that can be given with quite sufficient force without the slightest elevation of the point if the sword arm and leg act together.

In all other attacks and returns the feint, or the act of forming the guard, gives great impetus to the cut.

It has also been asserted that in making a thrust the sword moves in a straight line, and in making a cut it moves in a circle.

This assertion is erroneous, and having been made without contradiction, has been generally accepted as a fact, and hence become a popular error.

All straight thrusts and disengagements move in straight lines, but in the cut over, the point has to be drawn back before the thrust can be given, and when a cut over is made after a parry, the point traverses as great if not a greater distance than in any cut.

Compare the following movements, which I think are the longest made either in thrusting or cutting.

Engage with foils in quarte and parry the disengagement into tierce with prime, and riposte with a cut over.

Engage with sabres in high seconde, and, guarding an attack at the head with prime, return at the inside of the leg.

All direct cuts at the right side on any part from head to foot, from whatever guards they are made, move in as straight lines as any thrusts that can be given, and are consequently as quick.

In all other cuts the point moves in a circle.

However partial one may be to the thrust, and I acknowledge that I am one of its partisans, justice should be given to the cut, and although it may not in every instance be so quick or so fatal in its effect as the thrust; it has its advantages. Among others, it rarely passes, that is, goes by the object aimed at, without touching it, as the thrust will often do, more particularly when aimed at the arm or leg.

USEFUL HINTS.

Immediately you go on guard, touch your adversary's sword with yours, and retire out of distance to avoid a surprise. This is called "engaging."

Keep your eyes open and fixed upon your adversary, watching all his movements.

Hold yourself in as easy a manner as possible, particularly the sword arm.

Keep your knees well bent while setting to; you cannot longe quickly unless you do.

Move the feet lightly, and never drag them on the ground.

Be careful to always keep sufficient room behind you to be able to retire. Should your adversary try to drive you back, either attack him or threaten an attack.

While manœuvring, keep out of reach, and plan your attacks and deliver them immediately you are within distance, then recover to the position of guard whether you have succeeded or not.

Should your adversary guard your attack and return, form the necessary guard, and make a second attack without the slightest delay.

Do not hit at the same place more than twice in succession, but vary your attacks and returns very much.

After two or three exchanges, break away out of distance to steady yourself and plan your next movements. In making long phrases you get slow and out of form, and, consequently, are not likely to get a hit.

Always deliver your cuts with a true edge and with the centre of percussion, which is generally about seven or eight inches from the point. It is the most effective part of the sword to cut with, and will not jar the arm like a cut made with any other part of the blade.

Never press upon your adversary's blade after having delivered a cut or thrust, but recover as quickly as possible to guard the return. Should he press upon yours, disengage and return as quickly as possible.

Make all your cuts with the wrist; never throw your arm out of line, but always keep it in front of you.

The action of cutting at your opponent's left side (called the inside line), is something like that of throwing, and at his right side (outside line) like that of whipping.

Always keep in front of your opponent, never more to your right or left; should he do so, keep on your own ground, turning only so much as to enable you to have your right toes pointed to his. Let him move round as much as he likes: he will only tire himself and gain no advantage.

Keep the head and body erect and quiet in all positions.* If you lean forward on the attack, a man much shorter than yourself can thrust you through the head by simply retiring and straightening his arm, while your attack would not reach him. You also cannot recover quickly, as too much weight is thrown upon the front leg.

Avoid remaining on the longe and getting to close quarters, no true defence can be made when in-fighting.

If you remain on the longe, your adversary may easily and without any danger step forward with his left foot and seize the wrist of your sword arm with his left hand.† By always recovering to your guard such a manœuvre is avoided, and, if attempted, you may easily deliver a straight thrust as he steps forward.

Another reason why you should always recover to your guard after an attack is, if you remain on

---

* The advantages of this are fully and clearly shown by that justly celebrated fencer, Captain G. Chapman, in his "Sequel to Foil Practice."

† Although this would not be permitted in a duel, a man would not hesitate to do it in actual combat

the longe and your adversary retires one step, you cannot reach him; he has then the advantage of position, and will be able to attack you, while you can only act on the defensive.

If you can hit your adversary without feinting, do so, as it is more dangerous to make two motions than one.

Use judgment, study your opponent's play, and make no meaningless movements. An assault ought not to last longer than ten minutes. After that time, if you have fenced with energy and vigour, you lose your quickness and get out of form, and thereby contract slow and bad habits.

EXERCISES.

The following exercises may be practised by two advanced players. The hits and guards must be made as correctly, smartly, and as rapidly in succession as possible, taking it in turns to lead off. Care being taken not to move the left feet, and to strictly preserve the proper distance between you.

The following is an example of the way in which they should be gone through:—

We are both on guard, and in hitting distance.

I say, "You lead off."

Head, head, under right arm.

You then lead off at my head, which I guard and return with a longe at yours.

You recover, and guard your head, and then with a longe hit under my right arm, I guard.

We should then remain steady a few moments, you on the longe hitting under my right arm, I on guard defending my right side, to see if the positions of the sword arms, feet, and bodies are correct.

This should invariably be done at the finish of each exercise. It helps to keep you in form.

Another Example.

You say to me, " You lead off."

Feint head, and hit under right arm. Thrust at breast. Head.

I feint at your head, and cut under your right arm, which you guard, and longeing, return with a thrust at my breast.

I recover and parry it, then, with a longe, cut at your head. Both remain steady to see the positions.

1st *Exercise*.—Head. Head. Head.
2nd *do*.—Head. Head. Under right arm.
3rd *do*.—Head. Head. Outside leg.
4th *do*.—Head. Head. Left breast.
5th *do*.—Head. Head. Inside leg.

6th Exercise.—Feint head, hit under right arm. Thrust at breast. Head.

7th do.—Feint head, hit outside leg. Thrust at breast. Head.

8th do.—Thrust straight at breast. Head. Hit under right arm.

9th do.—Disengage with a thrust. Hit under right arm. Head.

10th do.—Head. Head. Hit under right arm. Thrust at breast. Head.

11th do.—Head. Head. Hit outside leg. Thrust at breast. Head.

12th do.—Feint a thrust under the blade, and hit at the head. Inside leg. Thrust at the breast. Head. Head.

In these exercises you must not get into the habit of cutting only at each other's swords, and thereby making a mock combat, but you should try to hit each other on every occasion.

THE SALUTE.

The Salute is a ceremony usually performed by two sabre-players previous to making an assault. It is a mark of respect to those looking on, and an act of courtesy to each other.

Both should move together, and keep correct time throughout its performance.

There is no established method, but the following is that generally adopted by the best sabre-players I know.

The two adversaries, facing each other in the first position, without wearing masks, which should be laid on the floor on their left, go smartly on guard, as shown in Plate II., and having beat twice on each other's blades, return to the first position.

Both bring the hilt to the mouth, the point of the thumb level with the lower lip, sword upright, and edge to the left. This is called "Recover swords." Then turning the face and directing the eyes to the left, slowly and gracefully extend the arm and the sword in the same direction until the point is level with the centre of the face and arm nearly straight, hand in quarte, and as high as the shoulder.

After a short pause both again recover swords, and, turning the face to the right, extend the hand in a similar manner to the right. Hand in tierce.

From there they recover swords, and, falling on guard, beat a double attack with the right foot (a beat with the heel and one with the flat of the foot in rapid succession). Then, bringing the left foot up to the right, recover swords, and lower the hand and sword slowly towards the right hip. Arm straight, palm down, and edge to the right.

RULES.

You must not attack until an engagement has been formed.

Touches on any part are counted good.

You must not hit after you are touched, but recover to the first position and acknowledge the hit.

After each hit, both men should go to their original ground, and form a fresh engagement before renewing the assault.

When a man leads off with proper quickness, the other should guard before returning. Should he not do so, the hit belongs to the one who led off.

When two men lead off together and both hit, neither hit is counted.

When the Remise or Redouble and Return are made together, the hit belongs to the one making the Return.

If the Stop Thrust is not made in sufficient time to prevent the attack being delivered, the hit counts to the one making the attack.

A hit is counted good after a disarmament, if given immediately after and before there is time to think.

DRESS FOR SABRE PLAY.

Although the figures in the preceding illustrations are shown without masks or pads, no practice ought ever to be made without them. The following is the dress usually worn.

A flannel shirt and trousers, shoes with soles of buff leather, without heels.

A stout leather jacket, arm guard, leather apron, leg guard on right leg, and a pair of shoulder pads, shaped like a milkman's yoke.

A strong helmet covered with leather on the top, with large ear guards, and the mask of strong wire with the meshes sufficiently small to prevent the point of the sabre passing through. A leather stock should also be worn round the neck.

When practising with sticks, the shoulder pad and arm guard may be dispensed with, and the hand ought to be protected with a buffalo hide hand guard.

Basket hilts are dangerous, as the point of the stick is apt to pass through them, and your hand may thereby be seriously injured.

PRACTICE SABRE.

The practice sabre should have a quill edge, which is the bluntest edge there is, and the point should be rounded off.

SABRE v. BAYONET.

WHILE writing on this subject, the fencing names of the parries will be used, viz. :—

        Prime   (Head Guard).
        Seconde (Outside Leg Guard).
        Tierce (Outside Guard).
        Quarte (Inside Guard).

In describing how to deal with a man armed with a rifle and bayonet, it will be necessary to explain his methods of attack and defence.

A bayonet should be used like a foil, but in consequence of its weight and general unwieldiness, the simple movements of the latter weapon can only be executed by it, and as the sabre, from its weight and shape, is similarly circumstanced, the two arms, in that respect, are on equal terms.

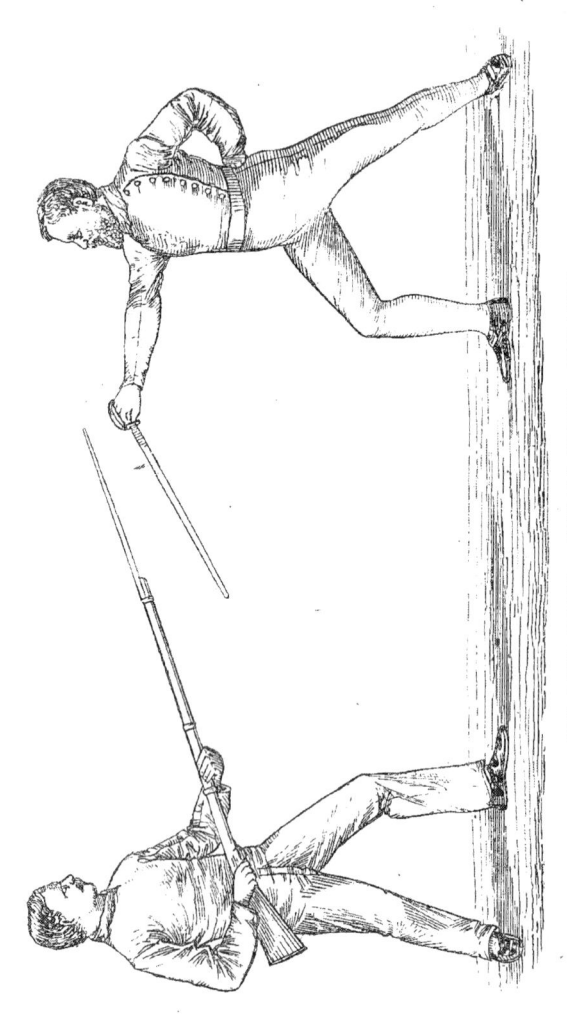

PLATE XXI.—ENGAGING GUARD.

PLATE XXI.

Engaging Guard.

A bayoneteer, therefore, engages in tierce or quarte, from which he can make the following attacks:—

A straight thrust.
A disengagement.
Feint a straight thrust and disengage.
"One, Two" (feint a disengagement into one line and disengage into another).

How to Parry his Straight Thrusts and Disengagements.

All his straight thrusts or disengagements over your blade may be parried with prime, and all those under your blade with seconde.

These parries are stronger than tierce and quarte, and are, therefore, better adapted for parrying such a heavy weapon as a rifle and bayonet.

They also defend the head and leg as well as the body, while the others only guard the breast.

Tierce and quarte may, however, be occasionally used against his thrusts at the breast. A greater variety of returns would be thereby obtained.

How to Parry, "Feint a Straight Thrust, and Disengage."

His feint of a straight thrust, when engaged under the blade and disengagement over the blade, may be parried with seconde and prime.

His feint of a straight thrust, when engaged over the blade and disengagement under the blade, may be parried with prime and seconde.

How To Parry "One, Two."

His "One, Two" below and above your blade may be parried with seconde and prime, and his "One, Two" above and below your blade with prime and seconde.

If he should deceive your quarte by feinting in quarte and thrusting in tierce, parry tierce.

If he deceive your tierce by "One, Two," parry seconde.

Should you at any time foresee that he is going to attack with "One, Two," do not answer the feint, but wait and parry his last movement.

Your parries, which should be made with the edge of the forte of the sword, must be close, and finished with firmness, without stiffness or too much force.

RETURNS.

The best returns from the different parries are the following, placed in the order of their comparative merits; but their application should greatly depend on the adversary's defence.

FROM PARRYING PRIME.

Straight thrust at breast (hand in tierce and opposite your right shoulder).

Cut at the left forearm.
    Do.   head (left diagonal).
    Do.   inside leg.

FROM SECONDE.

Thrust at breast over the guard (palm turned down).

Cut at the right side of the head, neck, or shoulder.
    Do.   left forearm.
    Do.   outside leg.
    Do.   inside leg.

PLATE XXII.—PARRY OF TIERCE.

PLATE XXII.

PARRY OF TIERCE.

From Tierce.

Thrust at breast under the guard (hand in tierce and opposite your right shoulder).
Cut at outside right forearm.
Do. head (left horizontal).
Do. do. (right diagonal).
Do. inside leg.

PLATE XXIII.—PARRY OF QUARTE.

PLATE XXIII.

PARRY OF QUARTE.

From Quarte.

Thrust under left arm (hand in quarte and opposite left shoulder).
Cut at left forearm.
  Do. head (right horizontal).
  Do. do. (left diagonal).
  Do. outside leg.

HOW TO ATTACK A MAN ARMED WITH A RIFLE AND BAYONET.

A man thus armed engages in quarte or tierce, but standing with his left foot in front, his quarte will be your tierce and his tierce your quarte; that is, his right side is his quarte and your right side is your tierce, and *vice versâ*.

He will parry attacks made at the right side of his head or body with quarte, and those made at the left side of the head or body with tierce.

He will defend the top of his head with prime

PLATE XXIV.—CUT, INSIDE OF WRIST AFTER FEINT AT HEAD TO DECEIVE PRIME.

and his leg with half-circle. In both of these guards his left arm is very much exposed.

The following attacks without a feint may be made :—

Cut at his left wrist.

Thrust straight when the line in which he is engaged is not closed.

Disengage with a thrust either from tierce to quarte or from quarte to tierce.

PLATE XXIV.

To Deceive his Prime.

Feint at head and thrust under his guard. (Hand in tierce and opposite your right shoulder.)

Ditto, and cut inside his left wrist (*vide* Plate XXIV.).

Ditto, ditto, inside his leg.

PLATE XXV.—CUT AT HEAD AFTER FEINT AT INSIDE LEG TO DECEIVE HALF-CIRCLE.

PLATE XXV.

TO DECEIVE HIS HALF-CIRCLE.

Feint at inside of leg, and thrust at left breast over the guard. (Hand in quarte and opposite your left shoulder.)

Ditto, and cut at his head (*vide* Plate XXV.).

Ditto, ditto, at his left wrist.

PLATE XXVI.—THRUST IN QUARTE AFTER FEINT IN TIERCE.
"ONE, TWO" TO DECEIVE TIERCE.

PLATE XXVI.

To Deceive his Tierce.

Feint a thrust in tierce (his left breast) and disengage with a thrust into quarte " One, Two." (Hand in tierce and opposite your right shoulder, *vide* Plate XXVI.)

Feint a cut at his left side and cut at his right.

Ditto, ditto, at his left cheek and cut at his right.

PLATE XXVII.—THRUST UNDER LEFT ARM AFTER FEINT IN QUARTE TO DECEIVE QUARTE.

PLATE XXVII.

To Deceive his Quarte.

Feint a thrust in quarte (his right breast) and disengage with a thrust in tierce " One, Two." (Hand in quarte and opposite your left shoulder.)

Feint a thrust in quarte, and disengage under his left arm " One, Two, Low." (Hand in quarte and opposite your left shoulder, *vide* Plate XXVII.)

Feint a cut at his right side and cut at his left arm.

Ditto at his right cheek and cut at his left.

All the above-named attacks may be preceded by a beat or an advance and beat.

The stop thrusts, time thrusts with opposition, remise, redouble, and reprise can be made upon you by a man armed with a gun and bayonet, and you can use them against him under the same circumstances as when opposed to a sabre.

To avoid his stop thrusts, you must adopt the methods recommended when opposed to a man who engages in tierce or quarte (*vide* page 78).

GENERAL OBSERVATIONS.

The bayoneteer has the longer weapon. You have the handier one. You must therefore use such tactics as will give it the advantage.

On taking guard, keep out of distance, and by feinting, endeavour to find out whether, if you attack him, he will parry or counter with a thrust, which some men, relying on the superior length of the rifle and bayonet, do when attacked.

If you think that the latter is his intention, make false attacks, as described in page 76, and draw out his thrust, which, having guarded, return with the greatest rapidity. A counter with a bayonet must be avoided by every means possible.

Should you see that he is disposed to guard, you may attack him without much fear of a counter.

You should not attack too often, but rely more upon your guard and quick return. When, however, you do attack, use the feints very much. Doing so gives the advantage to the handier weapon.

Your returns, in which the thrust should take a prominent part, must be made with the greatest rapidity, and the opposition in them, as in the attacks, strictly maintained, so that he cannot possibly deliver a remise thrust.

PLATE XXVIII.—HOW TO SEIZE THE RIFLE AFTER PARRYING PRIME.

PLATE XXVIII.

How to Seize the Rifle after Parrying Prime.

If you at any time have an opportunity of parrying his thrusts with your left hand, or of seizing the barrel of his rifle with it, do so. You must not then struggle and try to get it out of his hands, but must deliver a cut or thrust as quickly as possible. In an actual combat you would then have little difficulty in getting his weapon should you want it.

A good time to attempt this is when, after you have parried prime, he does not recover quickly to his guard. You should then step forward quickly with the left foot, and, seizing the rifle, pull it down and towards you, so that he cannot reverse it to strike you with the butt.

PLATE XXIX.—HOW TO SEIZE THE RIFLE AFTER PARRYING QUARTE.

PLATE XXIX.

How to Seize the Rifle after Parrying Quarte.

Or you may sometimes get hold of it after your parry of quarte, when he is slow in recovering. It will not then be necessary to step forward with the left foot, as your parry will almost send his weapon into your left hand.

Some men when thrusting leave go of the rifle with the left hand. When your adversary does this and you get hold of it, a quick and sudden pull will draw it out of his other hand, or perhaps pull him on his knees.

DRESS.

The dress should be the same as that worn when practising with sabres, except that the man using the bayonet should have the pad on his left leg, and both should wear a well-padded fencing or boxing glove on each hand.

ON SWORDS.

It will be useless for me to say anything about the length and shape of swords, as in the British, and, I believe, every other service, an officer, whether he belong to the army, the navy, or the reserve forces, is compelled to wear the regulation sword of the corps he belongs to.

He can, however, purchase it where he likes, and has a certain amount of discretion in small matters, which, if carefully attended to, may make a most important difference in the utility of his weapon. "Mony a mickle mak' a muckle."

I would advise him by all means to get it from a good sword cutler, and see the blade properly proved—a very necessary precaution, as no bad blade will stand so severe a test.

He may then be sure that there is no flaw in it or in the tang (the part that passes through the grip).

A flaw in either may cost you your life.

The blade should be stiff and not whippy, as a whippy blade meets with so much resistance from

SWORDS. 117

the air when cutting or guarding quickly, and the point should be light, so that the sword will feel well balanced in the hand.

A whippy blade with a heavy point wrenches the wrist and elbow joints, and is extremely difficult to use. It altogether mars the proper use of the weapon.

The grip should suit your hand, and the steel back should be roughened to prevent the sword from turning in it.

On service, the grip, if not too thick, may be lapped with thin string slightly waxed; by this means it may be altered to any shape you like, and you will be able to hold the sword more securely.

The sword should be tightly mounted, that is, the grip should not be loose, the blade well shouldered up both back and front, so that there is no space between the shoulder and the hilt, and the end of the tang securely screwed and rivetted at the pommel.

To test the mounting, strike both the back and edge of the blade several times sharply against a post. If the grip then remains firm and tight and the blade rings, it is a proof that the mounting is fairly good. Should it, after being used some time, become loose, have it put right at once.

You cannot give an effective cut with a loose-mounted sword. It stings your hand, and spoils the general handling of the weapon.

SCABBARD.

The scabbard should be lined with leather or laths of wood, and the mouthpiece with German silver, which is softer than steel, to preserve the edge when drawing and returning the sword.

EDGE.

Various edges are put on swords, but the best and most serviceable one, in my opinion, is a short chopper edge. It is the one put on swords used for cutting bars of lead, carcases of sheep and legs of mutton.

The bone of a leg of mutton, which is almost as hard as any substance the edge is likely to come in contact with, will not turn it.

I have now swords with this edge in my possession with which hundreds of bars of lead, numerous carcases of sheep and legs of mutton and other substances have been cut, and the edges are still in good condition and fit for use.

SOME REMARKS CONCERNING SWORD HILTS.

The shape of the grip in the regulation infantry sword is not bad generally, but the metal back is unnecessary, and is apt to cause the hand to slip.

The grip of Japanese swords, but for the fact of their having the curve presented the wrong way, strikes me as exceedingly good.

Were I having a fighting sword made to my own fancy, without regard to the regulation of any service, I should direct it to be made with a grip of shark's skin or leather, with a strong twist of wire wound round at half-inch intervals, as in the regulation pattern, but continued all the way round without any metal back.

The pommel should be considerably heavier than is customary, and the shell (and I consider this the most important thing) should be of a pattern differing materially from that in common use.

The present form of shell is carried out into a tolerably bold curve on the outer side, no doubt for the purpose of covering the knuckles and arm, which, in a right-handed man, are exposed on this side, while on the reverse side the shell does not project to quite half the same extent.

The consequence of this arrangement is that the greater weight on the outside tends to throw over,

I mean, to make the wrist rotate from left to right as it does in attacks on the inner line, and to make rotation correspondingly difficult on the outer line, that is, from right to left.

Now, it may be regarded as proved that attacks the inner line, although very effective, expose the swordsman more than those delivered at the outside of his adversary's body, consequently the tendency to which I have referred cannot but be considered a vicious one. Again, it may happen that the swordsman is disabled by a flesh wound sufficiently grave to incapacitate his sword arm, but not of such severity as to prevent his continuing in action should he have learned to use his left. If he then pass his sword into his left hand, he will find that the shell, as at present formed, offers a most inadequate protection to the hand and arm, which would not be the case if the projections were equal on both sides.

The Scotch basket hilt, with some modifications, so as to give freer play to hand and wrist, is not a bad pattern.

There should be little or no open work about the shell: an unlucky thrust or cut with the point might disable your hand.

I would also recommend that that part of the shell which comes into contact with the point of the thumb where it rests on the back of the grip should be lightly padded with a few thicknesses of soft leather, so as to lessen the concussion, which is sometimes of sufficient force to loosen your hold of the sword grip, or at all events to impair that nicety of touch upon which successful swordsmanship in a high degree depends.

Before leaving this subject, I should like to remark that, although the grip of the regulation sword is not so faulty as its shell, yet it appears to me capable of improvement.

The back of the grip is convex throughout its length, an arrangement which, when the thumb is pressed upon it, as it should be in the use of a light sabre, does not give so good a hold as one presenting in the lower part a concavity into which shall fit the convex surface of the extended thumb. I have in my possession a pair of practice sabres made upon this principle, and also with a squarer grip than is customary, which are delightful to handle.

SWORD FEATS.

PLATE XXX.—LEAD CUTTING (BEFORE DELIVERING THE CUT.)

SWORD FEATS.

PLATE XXX.

Lead Cutting.

To cut a bar of lead in two at one stroke.

This feat is sometimes called the "Cœur de Lion," deriving its name from the feat said to have been performed by Richard I. when he met Saladin the Saracen at the station of the Diamond of the the Desert, *vide* Sir Walter Scott's "Talisman."

It is one which every sabre-player ought to practise more or less. It teaches how to apply force and edge, and to finish your cuts with quickness, by which they are more effective. It also shows the power of a sword-cut when properly delivered.

The great secret of this, and most of the sword feats, is a free delivery, true edge, and striking the object with the part of the blade called the centre of percussion with great velocity.

The sword generally used for this purpose is

something like a naval cutlass, but longer and heavier.

The best sized sword for a man of average strength is one weighing 3¼ lbs., with a blade 1¾ inches wide and 31 inches long. The size and weight, however, depend a great deal upon a man's strength. A weak man would cut better with a smaller one, and a very powerful man would find a larger one more suitable. It greatly rests on the velocity you are able to give it.

The bar of lead, which you can cast yourself if you are provided with a melting pan and mould, should be about 12 inches long and triangular (equilateral) in shape with flat ends, so that you can stand it on one end.

It may be either suspended or stood on end on the top of a table or stool; I prefer the latter way, as it is not so steady when suspended.

A three-legged stool about 4 feet high, for a man of 5 feet 8 inches, with a level top 9 inches square, will be found as handy as anything for this purpose.

Place the bar of lead so that your sword will first strike the most acute angle (should the bar be not quite equilateral), then put yourself in the position of "guard," with the toes of the right foot in a line with the lead, and at such a distance that when you deliver the cut you will strike it with the centre of percussion of your sword.

Having taken your distance, throw your hand quickly back into the bend of the left arm or on to the left shoulder to get an impetus, and keeping both feet firm on the ground, deliver a horizontal cut from left to right as rapidly as possible, using the elbow and forearm freely, and throwing the weight of the body into the cut. Arm straight and point of the sword to your right front at the finish of the cut.

In cutting, the wrist should be well sunk, the upper knuckles turned up, and a firm grip of the sword maintained, particularly at the moment the sword strikes the lead.

The sword, with the edge leading, should not be turned in the slightest degree, but kept on a level line so that the cut will be perfectly horizontal.

When the lead is suspended, aim a little above, and when standing, a little below the middle.

It is dangerous for any one to stand on your right when you are practising this feat, as the pieces of lead sometimes fly to a considerable distance, and with great force.

A little tallow on your sword will show you what part of the blade you cut with, and will also slightly assist the cut.

The lead may be cut in several other ways, viz., from right to left, but as the hand turns in this cut, you must be careful to strike the bar before this occurs.

It may also be thrown up and cut while in the air, or it may be placed on a trestle about 3 feet high, and cut with a downward chop: the way in which Cœur de Lion is said to have cut the handle of a steel mace.

A good practice is also to place the lead at the distance your adversary would be from you were you having an assault, and make attacks upon it, or forming a guard, give the various returns in the manner you would on a real opponent.

In this practice the lead should be thin, say 3 inches in circumference, as the cuts must be made without drawing the hand back, you therefore do not get the same sweep and force as when cutting in the manner first described.

A bar of this size is quite thick enough for your first practice in lead cutting. When you can cut it well, and with ease and certainty, you may try one a little thicker.

You should not attempt to cut one that is too large and above your power; you will only jar your elbow and destroy your confidence.

When you can cut a bar measuring $1\frac{1}{2}$ inches on each side, you may attempt to cut the carcase of a sheep weighing 60 lbs. or a leg of mutton of 9 lbs., and when you can cut one measuring 2 inches on each side (6 inches in circumference), you may try your hand on a 90 lb. sheep or a 14 lb. leg of mutton.

In melting the lead, which should be pure and unadulterated with any other metal, see that your mould is dry, as the slightest damp will cause the hot lead to spurt into your face.

Before pouring it into the mould, clear the surface of the dross which you will constantly find on it.

PLATE XXXI.—CUTTING A SHEEP (AFTER DELIVERING THE CUT).

PLATE XXXI.

To Cut a Sheep in Two at One Stroke.

Get the carcase of a sheep dressed in the ordinary way, as you see them hanging in a butcher's shop before they are cut up into joints.

Suspend it on a gallows by the hind legs with the belly towards you, then standing with your right toes in a line with the spine of the sheep, and so near that the centre of percussion of your sword will reach the back bone, and aiming at the part where the butcher separates the neck from the loin, deliver your cut as at the lead.

Take care to throw the point of your sword to your right front as you finish the cut, or you will leave part of the flank uncut.

To Cut a Leg of Mutton in Two at One Stroke.

Hang a leg of mutton by the shank with the bone side to your left, so that your sword will strike it first, and aiming at the "pope's eye," deliver your cut as at the lead.

Be particularly careful to grasp your sword tightly, or the bone, which is exceedingly hard, may cause it to turn in your hand.

This is rather a risky feat, for the reason that you have so little space to cut at in order to make a good section.

If you cut too low you will find a second bone, which will probably prevent your sword passing through.

If you cut too near the shank, it will be a bad section.

Before cutting at the "pope's eye," you may cut a thin slice or two off the bottom.

See that the shank bone has not been broken. Butchers often break it. It would probably spoil your cut.

For this and the sheep use the lead-cutting sword, and take care that the gallows is firm.

PLATE XXXII.

To Cut a Broom-handle or Wand on Two Glasses of Water without Breaking the Glasses or Spilling the Water.

Take your lead-cutting stool and another of exactly the same height. Place a tumbler filled

PLATE XXXII.—CUTTING A BROOM HANDLE ON WINE GLASSES.

with water on the top of each, then lay an ordinary broom-handle on the glasses, so that the ends will rest on the inside edges, each end projecting about half an inch over the water.

With your lead-cutter deliver a downward chop with great suddenness and quickness, striking as near the centre as possible.

This feat may also be done with a thinner wand on two wine-glasses.

Or you may hang two loops of paper or strong thread on the edges of two sharp swords and suspend the wand on them.

TO CUT A SILK CUSHION IN TWO AT ONE STROKE.

Hang a silk cushion, stuffed with feathers or down, so high that the centre of it would be a few inches higher than the top of your lead-cutting stool, then, aiming at the most acute edge, deliver as at the lead. On account of the inconvenience caused by the escape of the feathers from the cushion when cut, this feat has of late years been left unperformed at public assaults-of-arms. The last time I saw it executed was many years ago by my esteemed friend, Mr. Alfred Shury, at that time one of the best swordsmen in London.

This and the following are the feats said to have been done by Saladin, when he met Richard Cœur de Lion in the Diamond of the Desert.

They consequently bear his name.

PLATE XXXIII.—CUTTING A VEIL.

PLATE XXXIII.

To Cut a Veil in Two at One Stroke.

Fold a veil neatly lengthways and lay it on the edge of the sword, almost close to the hilt.

Place your feet together, with your sword hand resting on the bend of the left arm, the edge of the sword turned up. Take two quick steps to your front, beginning with the left foot, and as you make the second, deliver an upward cut with a good edge, throwing the point of the sword high in the air, so that when the veil separates the two parts will have some distance to fall. A good effect will thus be produced.

At the finish of this cut, as in the lead cutting one, the arm should be brought straight.

The feat may also be done with a cambric or a silk handkerchief (the latter is very difficult), or with a kid glove or ribbon.

When ribbon (which should be very narrow) is used, have three or four colours, about a yard of each, and lay the whole on the sword at once.

After cutting them once, take all the pieces and cut them again. If they are thrown high they will somewhat resemble the coloured fire falling from a sky-rocket, and will have a very pretty effect.

Gauze is the best textile to practise with. Try to cut a yard of it into as many pieces as possible, always taking care to fold each piece lengthways before placing it on the sword.

When you can do this well, try something more difficult.

For this and the preceding feat you require a special sword called a handkerchief cutter. It should have the edge of and be kept as sharp as a razor.

The edge should be ground and set towards the hand, and when sharpening or stropping it, you should always rub from point to hilt.

If you look through a very powerful magnifying glass you will find the edge of a sword is serrated like a saw, but not so regularly; therefore, by having the teeth pointed towards the hilt, the edge more readily lays hold of the veil.

To understand this more clearly, take a common saw, whose edge is set towards the point, and rub your finger from handle to point. However hard you may press, the teeth will not prick you. Rub the other way and the effect will be very different.

To Cut a Sheet of Note-paper Unsupported.

Take a sheet of note-paper, and, half opening it, place it on end on the lead-cutting stool, the acute angle to your left, the opening to your right, and with your handkerchief cutter deliver as at the lead. This is not difficult.

In this and the preceding feats the thumb should be round the grip.

In the following it will be better to lay it on the back.

To Cut an Orange while Falling.

Suspend an orange by a piece of thin thread about four or five feet from the ground. Place yourself with the right toes in a line with the orange, then, with a very light touch of the sword near to the point, cut the thread, and quickly turning the hand, divide the orange as it falls.

The thread may be cut from right to left and the orange from left to right, or *vice versâ*, whichever you find the handier. In both ways the cuts must be very small and close.

For this and the following feats any light and handy sword will do. It should not be very sharp except close to the point, so that you can cut the thread with ease, and thus cause the orange to fall straight.

PLATE XXXIV.—CUTTING AN APPLE ON A MAN'S HAND.

PLATE XXXIV.

To Cut an Apple in Two on a Man's Hand Without Injuring Him.

This is called the "Napier Feat," from the fact that it was done on Sir Charles Napier's hand when in India by a native swordsman.

It is very dangerous and difficult, and none but those who have great command over a sword should attempt it.

The man who holds the apple should have good nerve, and should keep his hand very steady. He must raise the palm of his hand as much as possible, and, keeping the four fingers close together, bend them back. The thumb must also be pressed back, and kept as far as possible from the forefinger.

Place the apple on his palm, and standing so that your sword will pass between his thumb and forefinger and point in the same direction, deliver a downward cut without the slightest draw and with sufficient force and no more than will cut the apple.

This is such a delicate and dangerous feat that whenever I have to do it I practise on several apples of the sort I intend to cut, so that I may find out the exact force to apply. Apples differ so much in toughness.

To Cut an Apple in a Handkerchief Without Injuring the Latter.

Take a pocket-handkerchief and tie the four corners together with a piece of string. Hang it four or five feet from the ground, then put in the apple so that it will rest exactly in the centre.

Aiming under the apple, give an upward cut of sufficient force to pass through. If you make the slightest draw you will cut the handkerchief.

When apples cannot be got, you may use potatoes or thin-skinned turnips for this and the preceding feat.

When performing these feats, take great care that no one is within reach of your sword, and see that everything is properly placed and steady before delivering your stroke.

Do not chop or hack, but make the cuts with neatness and freedom. Avoid all parade, and always remember to grasp your sword so that the middle knuckles are in a line with the edge of the sword. This rule is imperative.

RULES OF
DUELLING WITH SABRES.

THE FOLLOWING ARE THE

RULES OF DUELLING WITH SABRES,

TRANSLATED FROM "ESSAI SUR LE DUEL,"

BY THE

COMTE DE CHATEAUVILLARD.

CHAPTER VII.

Duel with Sabres.

1st.—Each combatant must have two seconds for this sort of duel, and one of the two must have a sabre. They must, if possible, get sabres with curved blades for the two antagonists, as being less fatal.

2nd.—When arrived on the ground there must be no discussion between the two combatants, their seconds being their plenipotentiaries.

3rd.—The seconds having agreed upon the choice of the ground the most proper for the combat—level and equal for the two opponents—must mark the two places, the distance being calculated as if the two opponents were both on the longe and the points of the two sabres one foot apart.

4th.—The seconds, after having tossed for the places, take their principals to the place given to each by chance.

5th.—Gloves with gauntlets are generally used for this duel, but the seconds of the insulted party (if belonging to the class spoken of in the 11th sec. of the 1st chap.) can oblige the combatants not to wear them. Nevertheless, every one is entitled to wear an ordinary glove, or a pocket-handkerchief round the hand, but the handkerchief must not hang down.

6th.—If the insulted party (if belonging to the class spoken of in the 10th and 11th secs. of the 1st chap.) wishes to wear a glove with a gauntlet, his seconds must offer a similar one to his opponent, and if the latter refuses it, the insulted party may use his and the other wear an ordinary glove or handkerchief.

7th.—When the combatants are placed, the seconds measure the blades, which must be of equal length and similar shape. The choice of the sabre, if similar ones are used, must be tossed for. If by carelessness the sabres are not alike, the choice should still be tossed for; but if the sabres are too disproportioned for such a combat it should certainly be put off.

8th.—But, however, if the combatants belong to the same regiment they can use their own sabres, but the sabres must be mounted the same.

9th.—The insulted party (if in the class of 11th sec., 1st chap.) can use a sabre belonging to him, but he must offer a similar one to his adversary, who can refuse it and then use his own; nevertheless, if the difference should give a too great disadvantage to either one or the other the seconds should postpone the duel, unless the seconds of both parties present a pair of sabres unknown to the combatants. Then the choice of the pair should belong to the insulted party, and the choice of the sabre to the other.

10th.—The seconds, after having invited the combatants to take off their coats and waistcoats, must go up to their principal's opponent, who must show his naked breast in order to prove that he wears nothing to protect himself against the edge or point of the sabre blade. His refusal would be equivalent to a refusal to fight.

11th.—When what is above described is finished, the seconds should toss for which one of them is to explain the conventions of the duel to the combatants, to whom the weapons are then given, with the recommendation to wait until the signal is given to begin.

12th.—When the seconds are placed on both

sides of the combatants, the one designed gives the signal by the word—*Allez!*

13th.—If before the signal is given the combatants join blades together it is equivalent to a signal, but it is blamable if only one of the two does it.

14th.—When the signal is given the combatants can cut and thrust at one another, advance, retire, stoop, turn round, vault, and do anything they think profitable to them : such are the rules of the combat.

15th.—It is against the rules of this combat to strike your opponent when he is disarmed or when he is on the ground, to take hold of his arms or his body or to take hold of his weapon.

16th.—Disarmed means when the sabre has fallen out of the hand, or when dropping the point has touched the ground.

17th. — When one of the combatants is wounded his seconds must stop the combat until they think it proper that it should begin again.

18th.—If before there is any wound one of the seconds wishes to stop the duel, he asks if he can do so to the opposing seconds by lifting up his stick or sabre, and if an affirmative answer is given by the same movement he suspends the duel.

19th.—The seconds can agree beforehand to

stop the duel at the first blood shed—humanity and the gravity of the case must guide them.

20th.—If one of the two combatants is killed or wounded against the rules of the duel, the seconds must refer to the 20th and 21st art. of the 4th chap.

DUEL WITH SABRES WITHOUT THRUSTS.

1st.—If possible sabres with blunt points must be used for this duel.

2nd.—Each combatant must have two seconds.

3rd.—The seconds, after having agreed upon the choice of the ground best fitted for the combat—level and equal for the two opponents—must mark the two places at the distance calculated, as if the opponents were both on the longe and the points joining together.

4th.—Either combatant can use gloves with gauntlets provided the adversary has one too, or that a similar one can be offered to him, otherwise the difference must be levelled by the seconds.

5th.—The weapons must be alike and unknown to the combatants, but if the combatants belong to the same regiment they can use their own sabres, provided they are of the same sort and have the same mountings.

6th.—The seconds, after having tossed for the places, take their friends to the places which have fallen to them.

7th.—The seconds must toss for which of the two antagonists is to choose his sabre.

8th.—The second designed to give the signal must explain to the combatants the conventions of the duel, which are, that it is strictly forbidden to make use of the points of the sabres, which would be felony.

9th.—The seconds invite their friend to strip naked down to the waist, but they may keep their braces on if they are used to them.

10th.—The seconds present both sabres to the combatant who has gained by toss the right to choose, who picks one out, they then present the last one to the other combatant and recommend them both to wait for the signal.

11th.—When the seconds are placed on both sides of the combatants the signal is given by the word—*Allez !*

12th.—When the signal is given the combatants can cut at one another—taking care not to wound their adversary with the point of their sabre—can stoop, advance, retire, turn round, vault, &c., and stop only when the seconds tell them to: such are the rules of the combat.

13th.—The seconds must always stop the duel

as soon as one of the combatants is wounded, in order to see whether he can continue or not—the seconds are the only judges for that; but the custom in this kind of duel is to stop the combat at the first wound.

14th.—If one of the combatants is killed or wounded against the rules, *see* 20th and 21st art. of 4th chapter.

CHAPTERS 1st—10th.—The insulted party has the choice of the duel and weapons.

11th.—The insulted party, if struck or wounded, has the choice of the duel, weapons, distances, and can forbid his opponent to use weapons belonging to him, but in that case he must not use his own.

CHAPTERS 4th—20th.—The seconds must, if anything takes place against the rules, make a written statement of it and prosecute the felon by all the laws in their power (and *poursuivre le fauteur devant les tribunaux par toutes les voies de droit en leur pouvoir*).

21st.—The seconds of the party who is charged with felony must, by all means, declare the truth. They are not otherwise accountable for it, unless they aided in committing the wrong, which cannot be supposed possible.

Printed by Amazon Italia Logistica S.r.l.
Torrazza Piemonte (TO), Italy